To Luke, to whom I read first
—K. M.

To friends, family, editors, art
directors, agents: Your patience,
help, and understanding gave
me the opportunity to take one
huge step toward making this
book a reality
—R. F.

Published by Roaring Brook Press
Roaring Brook Press is a division of Holtzbrinck
Publishing Holdings Limited Partnership
120 Broadway, New York, NY 10271
mackids.com

Library of Congress Control Number: 2020912162
ISBN 978-1-250-22902-1

Our books may be purchased in bulk for promotional, educational, or business use. Please contact your
local bookseller or the Macmillan Corporate and Premium Sales Department at (800) 221-7945
ext. 5442 or by email at MacmillanSpecialMarkets@macmillan.com.

First edition, 2021
Book design by Elizabeth H. Clark
Printed in China by RR Donnelley Asia Printing Solutions Ltd., Dongguan City, Guangdong Province
The illustrations for this book were created digitally.
10 9 8 7 6 5 4 3 2 1

WE WAIT
for the
SUN

BY **Dovey Johnson Roundtree** AND **Katie McCabe**

PICTURES BY **Raissa Figueroa**

ROARING BROOK PRESS · NEW YORK

The girl in this story, DOVEY JOHNSON ROUNDTREE, was born more than one hundred years ago in Charlotte, North Carolina. During a time of racial inequity in America, she grew up to become a legendary civil rights lawyer, fighting for justice. No matter how dangerous the fight was, she refused to quit. She believed that a better day was coming for African American people, because that was what she had been taught by her bold and brave grandmother, Rachel Bryant Graham. Dovey loved to tell stories of her Grandma Rachel. The story Dovey loved best is the one you are about to read.

In the hour before dawn, we slip out of the house, and the midsummer night is dark and cool.

As I follow the
swish,
swish
of my grandmother's skirts, I can smell
the damp earth beneath my feet and feel
the dewy air on my face.

Moving through the darkness toward the woods where blackberries grow, I'm certain Grandma Rachel and I are the only ones awake in the whole world.

But then, as if by some secret signal, the others appear in
doorways and fall into line one by one behind us.

By daylight, these are the grown-up ladies who come to quilt with Grandma, passing food over the fence, gathering in our backyard for soapmaking. But now they are just shadowy figures in our silent march, our secret mission, our berry picking.

It grows cooler as we enter the forest, and darker.
"Dovey Mae?" Grandma calls out.

"I'm right here," I answer. "Right over here."

"The darkness isn't anything to be afraid of, child. If you wait just a little, your eyes will learn to see, and you can find your way. Hold on to my apron, now."

We begin to walk. Grandma's steps are swift
and sure, and I move as she does. I fix my eyes
on the shiny heels of her shoes, and I listen.

The darkness holds a thousand sounds. As we push deeper
and deeper into the woods, the blackness turns to gray,
and sleepy birds begin calling to each other, sending
echoes
through
the treetops.

Grandma says the birds'll lead you to the best berries, every time.
Sure enough, as we follow the sound of beating wings just ahead,
we come into a clearing ringed with berry-studded bushes.

The ladies swoop down, pails clanging, but I move closer to
Grandma, following the sweep of her hand as it grazes a bush
and comes back with the first berry of the day, frosted with dew.

I open my mouth, she drops in the berry, and I bite down hard and suck the juice and know that there is no blackberry anywhere like this one, so fat it squirts seedy blue juice down my overalls and so sweet I keep licking my lips to get the taste.

Grandma looks down at me and laughs. Then she turns to the bushes and starts to hum, the way she does when it's time to get to work.

The clearing fills with the sound of berries
hitting tin pails. From my spot in the bushes I
pick berries as fast as I can and listen to the
w h i s p e r s
of the goings-on at church.

Already, heat is rising from the forest floor, making me think of the feast that is coming in just a little while, of how I'll eat berries from the minute I get home to the minute I go to bed.

Again and again, Grandma reaches low or stands tiptoe to pluck berries. And then, suddenly, in the middle of her rush, she stops.

"Look, Dovey Mae," she whispers. "Over yonder."

Slowly, slowly, the horizon pinkens.

"Here she comes!"
Grandma whispers. She draws me to her, and together we
watch the pink turn to red, the red to gold.

Then, all at once, as if at my grandmother's command, the orange ball that is the sun shows its face.

It rises up over the edge of the world, and as it does, Grandma rises, too, and stands, just looking, her face shining in the light.

I don't know how long we stay there watching, but when Grandma claps her hand on my shoulder and shakes out her skirts, dawn is day.

My grandmother turns and heads down the path, quick and hurried again, leading me home.

When I think of Grandma, I see her there, standing in the clearing, pail and sack at her feet, face upturned to meet the dawn.

Always, I see her
waiting
for
the sun.

AUTHOR'S NOTE

When I met Dovey Roundtree in 1995, she was eighty-two years old, and I was immediately drawn to her strength and her fierce passion for justice. A childhood story about pre-dawn blackberry picking may seem an odd choice to represent the life of a civil rights icon of Dovey's magnitude. But in the twelve years she and I worked together on her autobiography, *Mighty Justice*, I came to understand that no relationship in her vast experience went more to the core of her soul than the one she had with her grandmother. In an era when the Ku Klux Klan terrorized Black communities and Jim Crow laws told Black children they were inferior, Dovey's grandmother, Rachel, imbued her with the certainty of her self-worth, giving her the most precious gift of all: her time. In the magical hour just before dawn, when Dovey was abroad with Grandma Rachel, she drank in the beauty of the universe in all its infinite possibility, and she did so in the presence of an adult she adored, and who loved her fiercely. This, without a doubt, shaped her into the woman she became. In its very ordinariness, it was life-altering.

We Wait for the Sun was adapted from the final chapter of the autobiography Dovey and I wrote together. I am sorry that she did not live to see the publication of this picture book, because she believed so deeply in our obligation to young people. From every pulpit to which she was given access in the final years of her life, she spoke of the need to sustain and nurture the next generation. With Dovey, this nurturing was far more than an abstract cause. Though she had no children of her own, she had a godson—James Andrew Pritchett, son of her beloved goddaughter, Charlene Pritchett-Stevenson—whom she cared for with the intensity of a grandparent. She looked at every child who crossed her path in terms of his or her potential, and in the twenty-three years I knew Dovey, I never once saw her pass up a child. That is how I know she would have loved this book. It is for the children. And it is for the adults who teach and nurture them, that all of them may come to understand that there is nothing more life-shaping than the moments between a parent or grandparent and a child.

May every child and adult who reads *We Wait for the Sun* bask in the glow of Dovey Roundtree's spirit, and that of her beloved Grandma Rachel, who in the midst of a world filled with pain and danger, believed with her whole heart in the dawn.

—Katie McCabe

DOVEY MAE JOHNSON ROUNDTREE (1914–2018) and RACHEL MILLIS BRYANT GRAHAM (1872–1964)

Groundbreaking lawyer, minister, and army veteran Dovey Johnson Roundtree was born in Charlotte, North Carolina, in 1914, in the midst of racial violence and rigid division of the races. The segregation system known as Jim Crow, mandated by the notorious 1896 Supreme Court ruling *Plessy v. Ferguson*, forced Black Americans in the southern states to live apart from white people, to attend separate schools, to drink from separate water fountains, and to sit apart from whites on trains and buses. The slogan of Jim Crow was "separate but equal," but Black men and women in the South knew it was anything but. Those who spoke out against segregation risked severe retaliation, even death, at the hands of the Ku Klux Klan, whose power peaked during the years of Dovey's childhood. One of her earliest memories was of hiding beneath her grandparents' kitchen table with her mother and three sisters while a horde of Klansmen on horseback galloped through the neighborhood.

In a world filled with fear and danger, Dovey looked to her grandmother, Rachel Millis Bryant

Dovey Johnson Roundtree, July 1914, on the occasion of her baptism at Charlotte's East Stonewall AME Zion Church by her grandfather, Rev. Clyde L. Graham.

Graham (1872–1964), as a bastion of strength. Born to former slaves, "Grandma Rachel," as Dovey called her, came of age during the tumultuous period called Reconstruction.[1] When Rachel was just thirteen years old, a white overseer on the farm where her father worked broke her feet after she rejected his advances. She limped all her life. After she lost her first husband to the ravages of the Klan, Rachel married Rev. Clyde L. Graham, pastor of East Stonewall African Methodist Episcopal Zion Church in Charlotte, North Carolina, where the two made their home. It was to that home that Grandma Rachel brought Dovey's mother and three sisters following the death of Dovey's father in the 1919 influenza epidemic. There, Dovey learned the lessons in self-worth, faith, and courage that would define her lifelong battle for justice.

When Dovey was six years old and riding the trolley into downtown Charlotte with her grandmother, the driver lashed out at her when she took a front seat reserved for white people. Outraged, Grandma Rachel disembarked from the trolley and, taking Dovey by the hand, headed into town on foot as trolley after trolley passed them by. Dovey would always remember that long, silent walk, and her grandmother's declaration when she recounted the incident that night to the entire family, that her children were "as good as anybody." As Dovey grew older, Grandma told her the story of her childhood and why she limped so badly. Each evening, she would bathe her feet and rub them with a salve she made of turpentine

Dovey Johnson Roundtree's maternal grandmother, Rachel Bryant Graham, circa 1915. Dovey identified her as the single most important influence in her life.

and mutton tallow, to relieve the aching muscles so she could walk the next day. For Dovey, who loved to help her grandmother with this ritual, the image of Grandma's gnarled, misshapen feet became a lifelong symbol of both racial injustice and bold resistance.

Grandma Rachel was more than the centerpiece of just her own family. As an early member of the NAACP,[2] an officer in the Order of the Eastern Star, and the wife of a minister, she occupied a revered position in Charlotte's African American community. She was even sought out by activist, college president, and presidential adviser Mary McLeod Bethune, whom she entertained in her home during Bethune's recruiting trips for the National Association of Colored Women's Clubs. In introducing Dovey to Bethune, Rachel Graham placed her granddaughter within the orbit of one of the most powerful Black women in America.

Bethune's example inspired Dovey to set her sights on the prestigious Spelman College, one of the first universities for Black women in the country. Working three jobs in order to pay her tuition, and assisted by a loan from a white professor named Mary Mae Neptune, Dovey graduated from Spelman in 1938 and took a teaching job in Chester, South Carolina. At the outbreak of World War II, Dr. Bethune selected Dovey for a historic spot in the first class of Black women in the military. At the time, neither women nor people of color of either gender were welcome in the

---

1 Reconstruction was the twelve-year period following the American Civil War in which efforts were made to rebuild after the death and destruction of the war and to rectify the injustice of slavery—amid rampant violence from white southerners and terror groups like the Ku Klux Klan.

2 The National Association for the Advancement of Colored People, an organization founded in 1909, focused on political, educational, social, and economic equality and eliminating race-based discrimination.

Captain Dovey Johnson Roundtree addressing potential WAC recruits, Akron, OH, 1944.

armed services, but Bethune, with the assistance of First Lady Eleanor Roosevelt, cracked the wall of discrimination and made a path for Black women in the military. In May 1942, Dovey entered the first Officer Candidate School of the newly formed Women's Army Auxiliary Corps (later the Women's Army Corps, or WAC), one of forty African American women to hold that distinction.

Commissioned in August 1942 as a third officer, Dovey rose to the rank of captain and became a force for recruiting other Black women into the army—even as she risked court martial by defying Jim Crow laws in the military. Dovey would later point to this period as the beginning of her public battle for justice. When she met lawyer and activist Pauli Murray during her postwar employment with labor leader A. Philip Randolph, she was inspired to enroll in Howard University School of Law in Washington, DC, in 1947. At Howard, legal giants Thurgood Marshall and James Madison Nabrit Jr. were leading the NAACP Legal Defense Fund team in the charge against *Plessy v. Ferguson* that would culminate in the momentous 1954 school desegregation case *Brown v. Board of Education*. Howard Law School, the premiere legal training institution for African Americans, was a hotbed of civil rights activism, and Dovey threw herself into the battle.

In Dovey's war on racial discrimination, Grandma Rachel became her first client. Dovey and her law partner, Julius Winfield Robertson, filed a lawsuit in 1950 against the Southern Railroad for forcing Grandma and Dovey's mother, Lela Bryant Johnson, to stand for the entire ride from Charlotte when they traveled to Washington, DC, as first-class ticketed passengers to attend Dovey's law school graduation. The monetary settlement was so small that Dovey vowed she would stop at nothing after that to win justice for Black people in America. In November 1955, she and Robertson won a landmark bus desegregation case before the Interstate Commerce Commission on behalf of a Black army private named Sarah Keys, who had been thrown off a North Carolina bus for refusing to yield her seat to a white marine. That ruling, *Sarah Keys v. Carolina Coach Company*, handed down three weeks before Rosa Parks took her historic stand in Montgomery, Alabama, was the only explicit rejection of the *Plessy v. Ferguson* "separate but equal" doctrine by any court or administrative body in the field of interstate bus transportation.

Dovey Johnson Roundtree, circa 1985, on the steps of US District Court for the District of Columbia.

Rev. Dovey Johnson Roundtree, circa 1980, at an AME Church conference in Memphis, TN.

In 1961, *Keys v. Carolina Coach* became the centerpiece of Attorney General Robert F. Kennedy's battle to end Jim Crow in travel across state lines during the Freedom Riders' campaign.[3] The *Keys* case accomplished in interstate bus travel what Rosa Parks accomplished in city bus travel during the Montgomery Bus Boycott.

Despite the sudden death of her partner Julius Robertson in November 1961, Dovey continued to practice law alone, and the following year she became the first Black member of the Women's Bar Association of the District of Columbia, amid a firestorm of controversy. In 1970, she founded the law firm of Roundtree Knox Hunter & Parker. All her life, Dovey remembered the lessons Grandma Rachel had taught her about being brave and walking into the darkness even in the midst of fear.

Grandma Rachel, who urged Dovey to study for the ministry two years before the AME Church ordained women, lived to see her granddaughter become an ordained itinerant deacon in 1961, and she celebrated the beginning of Dovey's ministry at Allen Chapel AME Church in Washington, DC.

On November 1, 1964, Grandma Rachel died at the age of 91 just as Dovey was embarking on the most famous murder defense case of her career. In the midst of her grief, Dovey drew on Grandma's strength and wisdom to win an acquittal for the young Black man named Ray Crump, accused of murdering JFK mistress Mary Meyer. The victory vaulted her to prominence, and she went on to earn a reputation as one of Washington's most formidable criminal defense attorneys. In her final years, Dovey took on the cause of children, calling for an end to what she called "the demon of violence." Even after her retirement to Charlotte in 1996, she continued her impassioned call to parents and grandparents to save the next generation. Because of her grandmother, she told her audiences, she never stopped believing that a better day was dawning.

As a Black woman who shattered barriers in the law, the military, and the ministry, Dovey experienced cruelty and scorn, but at every step she moved forward to make history. She was honored by the American Bar Association in 2000 with its Margaret Brent Women Lawyers of Achievement Award; by the Association of Black Women Historians in 2009 for the autobiography she co-authored with Katie McCabe, *Justice Older Than the Law* (reissued in 2019 as *Mighty Justice*); and by the Women's Bar Association of the District of Columbia in 2011 with its Janet B. Reno Torchbearer Award. In 2013, a senior living facility in Southeast Washington was named "The Roundtree Residences" in her honor.

Dovey Johnson Roundtree died on May 21, 2018, at the age of 104. Her funeral service took place at Charlotte's East Stonewall AME Zion Church, where she had been baptized by her grandfather as a three-month-old child.

---

3 A campaign organized by the Congress of Racial Equality (CORE) wherein Black and white civil rights activists, mostly students, rode interstate buses together into the South to protest segregation in bus terminals, facing violence and arrests at every turn.

TIMELINE

1861–1865: The Civil War

1865–1877: Reconstruction Period ends remnants of slavery with passage of 13th, 14th, and 15th Amendments amid resistance by the Southern states and terrorism by Ku Klux Klan.

1872: Rachel Millis is born in Greensboro, North Carolina, to former slaves Lewis and Laura Crowe Millis.

1896: Supreme Court makes "separate but equal" the law of the land in *Plessy v. Ferguson.*

1914: On April 17, Dovey Mae Johnson is born in Charlotte, North Carolina, to AME Zion Church printer James Eliot Johnson and domestic Lela Bryant Johnson. She is baptized by her grandfather, Rev. Clyde L. Graham, pastor of East Stonewall AME Zion Church.

1914–1918: World War I

1919–1920: Influenza pandemic kills 50 to 100 million people worldwide. Dovey's father, James Eliot Johnson, dies of influenza in 1919.

1929–1939: The Great Depression

1934–1938: Dovey works her way through Spelman College, taking a teaching job in Chester, South Carolina, upon graduation in 1938.

1941: United States enters World War II.

1942: Mary McLeod Bethune selects Dovey as one of forty Black women to train as officers in the newly created Women's Army Auxiliary Corps (later the Women's Army Corps, or WAC).

1945: World War II ends. Dovey is discharged from the WAC and marries William A. Roundtree. She is inspired to enroll in law school.

1947–1950: Dovey, divorced from William Roundtree, attends Howard Law School on the GI Bill, one of five women in her class.

1954: On May 17, the Supreme Court unanimously strikes down the *Plessy v. Ferguson* rule of "separate but equal" in public education in *Brown v. Board of Education.*

1955: On November 7, Dovey and law partner Julius Winfield Robertson win a historic case, *Sarah Keys v. Carolina Coach Company*, to desegregate interstate buses, accomplishing in interstate bus travel what *Brown v. Board* did in public education.

On December 1, Rosa Parks is arrested for refusing to give up her seat to a white passenger on a city bus in Montgomery, Alabama. The resulting bus boycott vaults Rev. Martin Luther King Jr. to national prominence.

1961: During the Freedom Riders' campaign, Attorney General Robert F. Kennedy invokes *Keys v. Carolina Coach* in a Justice Department petition to the ICC, which enforces *Keys* six years after its initial ruling.

Dovey makes ecumenical history as one of the first women ordained to the ministry in the African Methodist Episcopal Church. She joins the staff at Allen Chapel AME Church in Washington, DC.

1962: Dovey becomes the first Black member of the Women's Bar Association of the District of Columbia.

1964: On November 1, Rachel Millis Bryant Graham dies.

1965: In *US v. Ray Crump*, Dovey wins acquittal for a Black laborer accused of the murder of a JFK mistress, securing a reputation as one of Washington's premiere criminal defense lawyers.

1970: Dovey founds the law firm of Roundtree Knox Hunter & Parker.

1996: Dovey retires, moves to Charlotte, and begins work with Washington writer Katie McCabe on her autobiography, *Justice Older Than the Law.*

2018: On May 21, Dovey Johnson Roundtree dies in Charlotte at the age of 104.

BIBLIOGRAPHY

Barnes, Catherine A. *Journey from Jim Crow: The Desegregation of Southern Transit*. New York: Columbia University Press, 1983.

Bell-Scott, Patricia. *The Firebrand and the First Lady: Portrait of a Friendship: Pauli Murray, Eleanor Roosevelt, and the Struggle for Social Justice*. New York: Alfred A. Knopf, Inc., 2016.

Janney, Peter. *Mary's Mosaic: The CIA Conspiracy to Murder John F. Kennedy, Mary Pinchot Meyer, and Their Vision for World Peace*, Second Edition. New York: Skyhorse Publishing, 2013.

McCabe, Katie. "She Had a Dream." *Washingtonian Magazine*, March 2002.

McCabe, Katie and Stephanie Y. Evans, "The Life of Dovey Johnson Roundtree (1914–2018): A Centenarian Lesson in Social Justice and Regenerative Power," pp. 121–140, *Black Women and Social Justice Education: Legacies and Lessons*. Albany, NY: SUNY Press, 2019.

McCluskey, Audrey Thomas and Elaine M. Smith. *Mary McLeod Bethune: Building a Better World: Essays and Selected Documents*. Bloomington, IN: Indiana University Press, 1999.

Putney, Martha. *When the Nation Was in Need: Blacks in the Women's Army Corps During World War II*. Metuchen, NJ: Scarecrow Press, 1992.

Robertson, Ashley N. *Mary McLeod Bethune in Florida: Bringing Social Justice to the Sunshine State*. Charleston, SC: The History Press, 2015.

Roundtree, Dovey Johnson, Papers, National Archives for Black Women's History of the Mary McLeod Bethune National Historic Site, Museum Resource Center, Landover, MD.

Roundtree, Dovey Johnson and Katie McCabe. *Mighty Justice: My Life in Civil Rights*. New York: Algonquin Books of Chapel Hill, 2019.